Through the Gates of Goodness

Discovering the Transformative Power of Virtue

A Modern Translation

Adapted for the Contemporary Reader

James Allen

Table of Contents

Preface - Message to the Reader

Rebuilding the Greatest Library in Human History

Thousands of years ago, the Library of Alexandria was the heart of global knowledge — a sanctuary where the wisdom of every known civilization was gathered and shared freely.

And then, it was lost.

Now, we're rebuilding it — and you are invited to join us.

At the Library of Alexandria, we've set out to make every book available to *every person on Earth* — not just in print, but in every language, every format, and for every reader.

Here's how we do it:

- **Deluxe Print Editions at True Printing Cost** - Order any book as a high-quality paperback, elegant hardcover, or stunning boxset — and only pay what it costs to print. No markups. No middlemen.
- **Unlimited Access to the Greatest Works** - Enjoy thousands of timeless classics — from Plato to Shakespeare to Tolstoy — in beautiful, modern eBook and audiobook editions. Read and listen without limits — for every reader, everywhere.
- **Modern Translations for Every Language & Dialect** - We're reimagining the classics in clear, accessible language — and translating them into every dialect imaginable. Everyone deserves to understand humanity's greatest ideas.

When you visit **LibraryofAlexandria.com**, you're not just accessing books — you're joining a global movement to restore, preserve, and share the wisdom of civilization.

Join us today at LibraryofAlexandria.com

Together, we'll ensure the light of human wisdom never fades again.

With gratitude,
The Modern Library of Alexandria Team

Visit:

www.libraryofalexandria.com

Or scan the code below:

Introduction

James Allen's Spiritual Compass:
The Quiet Strength of Virtue

Through the Gates of Goodness is a luminous work by James Allen, a spiritual philosopher best known for his classic As a Man Thinketh. While that short book gave the world a simple but powerful equation—thought shapes character and destiny—Through the Gates of Goodness builds upon that foundation by exploring a deeper truth: that true transformation, and with it true peace, can only be attained through the active cultivation of moral virtue. Written in Allen's signature contemplative style, this text takes readers on an inward journey, encouraging them to leave behind selfishness, illusion, and turmoil, and to enter instead a life shaped by gentleness, truth, compassion, and moral strength.

As with all of Allen's writings, this work reflects his conviction that human beings are not helpless victims of circumstance, but creators of their own lives—shaped by the thoughts they choose, the values they embody, and the conduct they practice. But Through the Gates of Goodness is especially significant in the James Allen corpus because it does not speak merely of personal success or mental power. Instead, it places virtue at the very center of spiritual progress. Here, goodness is not a vague ideal but a disciplined practice, a gateway to higher consciousness and lasting happiness.

Written during the later years of Allen's life, Through the Gates of Goodness reads like a sage's final guidance to those who genuinely seek self-mastery. Gone is the language of ambition or achievement. In its place, we find the calm voice of a soul who has walked the hard road of self-discipline and discovered a truth too often neglected in modern life: that peace and power arise not from outer conquest, but from inner goodness. Not from gaining more, but from becoming more.

For Allen, goodness is not sentimentalism. It is a courageous state of being. It demands clarity of thought, purity of motive, constancy of purpose, and gentleness in action. It means the absence of cruelty, the presence of truth, and the surrender of self-will to higher ideals. He reminds the reader that real strength lies not in dominating others, but in overcoming one's own lower nature. Those who pass "through the gates of goodness" are not weak—they are the strongest of all, for they have conquered the hardest enemy: themselves.

This modern edition is a faithful rendering of Allen's message, adapted for contemporary readers while retaining his voice and spirit. The language has been gently updated for clarity, but his core teachings remain untouched. They remain as powerful and relevant today as when they were first penned—perhaps even more so, in an age marked by distraction, disconnection, and the erosion of ethical foundations.

Allen's voice in this book is not the loud voice of reform or revolution, but the quiet voice of transformation. He speaks not to the crowd but to the individual. He does not offer systems or ideologies, but simple, eternal truths. The reader is not urged to change the world, but to change themselves—and by doing so, to begin changing the world in the only way that truly matters: through example.

To read Through the Gates of Goodness is to encounter a clear, uncluttered vision of what it means to live well. It is not a book for those seeking shortcuts or superficial rewards. It is a book for the sincere, the humble, the brave—those who are willing to look within, to face their own weaknesses, and to walk the lifelong path of self-refinement. For these readers, James Allen offers a map, a mirror, and a quiet blessing.

The Moral Pathway: Goodness as a Practical Power

James Allen insists, throughout this work, that goodness is not merely desirable—it is necessary. Without goodness, he argues, there is no real peace, no enduring joy, no true freedom. Virtue is not a luxury for saints or philosophers, but a practical necessity for every human being who wishes to live a fulfilled life. And contrary to modern assumptions, Allen believes that virtue is not weak, naïve, or outdated. It is the very essence of strength, wisdom, and forward progress.

For Allen, virtue is not measured in abstractions. It is demonstrated in action, in the consistent daily expression of honesty, patience, compassion, purity, courage, and humility. Each virtue is a gateway, a threshold through which the soul must pass to rise from confusion and sorrow into clarity and joy. To be good, in Allen's sense, is not to be morally superior. It is to be inwardly whole, unshaken by temptation, and devoted to the welfare of others as much as to one's own integrity.

A central theme in this book is that virtue must be consciously chosen. No one drifts into goodness. It requires effort, attention, and sacrifice. Selfishness must be unlearned, habits of thought must be reshaped, and emotions must be purified through reflection and self-control. Allen likens the process to cultivation: the soul is a garden, and only through continuous care can its flowers bloom. Without vigilance, weeds of vanity, resentment, and laziness will choke the growth of character.

The modern reader might find this demanding. But Allen is unwavering in his conviction that there is no higher work than the cultivation of one's own soul. All progress—whether in business, art, relationships, or community—must begin with the individual's moral strength. Without this foundation, all other achievements are hollow.

He also addresses the illusion of external causes. Much of modern life blames suffering on external conditions—other people, luck, politics, or society. But Allen redirects our gaze inward. Circumstances, he argues, are reflections of character. The outer life is shaped by the inner life. One who lives with gentleness will encounter less conflict. One who lives with honesty will attract trust. One who radiates patience and calm will diffuse anger and strife. Thus, to improve our outer life, we must refine our inner being. This is the gate through which we must pass.

The transformation Allen describes is not immediate, but gradual. It unfolds through practice and perseverance. The reader is encouraged to start with one virtue—say, honesty—and commit to it wholly. From there, other virtues can be added, like bricks building a temple. Eventually, the soul becomes a place of peace, strength, and joy—not because the world has changed, but because the person has changed their relationship to it.

Allen's understanding of goodness is also deeply relational. A good person, he says, brings peace to others. They do not provoke or manipulate. They do not deceive or control. Their presence is uplifting, their speech is healing, their actions are beneficial. To embody goodness is to become a beacon—a living demonstration of what is possible when a person lives by principle rather than impulse.

The Reward of the Virtuous Life

While much of modern self-help is focused on outcomes—wealth, health, influence—James Allen focuses on something far deeper: peace. Not just the absence of conflict, but the presence of a radiant stillness that can only be found when the soul is fully aligned with truth. This is the final promise of Through the Gates of Goodness. That the practice of virtue, difficult though it may be, leads not to ascetic denial, but to an abundant inner life.

Allen teaches that the truly good person is not only strong and free, but joyful. Their mind is not tormented by guilt or fear. Their relationships are not poisoned by deceit. Their path is not darkened by regret. They walk in the light because they live in harmony with the eternal laws that govern life. This harmony is not dictated by any religion or dogma—it is revealed through conscience, through reflection, through direct experience.

He is clear, however, that the way is narrow. Few will walk it. Many will be distracted by ease, pride, ambition, or cynicism. But to those who persevere, the reward is immense. They gain not only peace but wisdom—not only character but clarity. They are able to see life as it truly is, without distortion or fear. And this seeing, this insight, becomes its own reward.

In Allen's world, success is redefined. It is not the accumulation of things, but the expression of truth. It is not dominance over others, but mastery over the self. It is not fame or approval, but freedom from inner conflict. This vision may seem quaint to the modern mind, conditioned by constant stimulation and external benchmarks. But its power is undeniable. It cuts through the noise and reveals what really matters.

Allen's final encouragement is for each person to begin. No matter the past, no matter the present confusion, the gates of goodness stand open. They do not require perfection—only sincerity. Even the smallest step toward virtue is a step toward peace. Even the smallest act of kindness is a gesture toward freedom. The journey may be long, but the direction is clear.

To read Through the Gates of Goodness is to be reminded of the sacred possibility of the human soul. It is to remember that greatness is not found in outward stature but in inward integrity. And it is to hear, perhaps faintly at first, the still, small voice calling each of us to a better, truer, more luminous life.

In this modern edition, that voice has been preserved, its language gently refreshed, its rhythm retained. Let it speak to you now—not with pressure or urgency, but with quiet strength. The gates of goodness are before you. Step through.

Chapter 1
The Gate and the Way

The gate to Life is narrow, and the path is difficult, and only a few people find it. —Jesus

A good person, from the goodness in their heart, brings out good things. —Jesus

The highest goal of all religions is to teach people how to live, and both learning how to live and actually living it are what religion is all about. Purifying the human heart, building a life free of blame, and perfecting the soul are the key factors in every religion and belief system around the world. The essential part of every religion is the effort to practice Goodness, and everything else is just extra or unnecessary. Goodness—and by this, I mean living without sin—is the beautiful and lasting form of Religion, while creeds and beliefs are like clothes that people use to dress it up, but these clothes are made from opinions and will eventually fade away. Religions come and go, but Religion, which is Life itself, lasts forever. People should stop arguing about the "clothes" and start understanding the universal beauty of the inner form, and by doing this, they will

11

unite with the supreme Goodness. Religion is Goodness, and Goodness is Religion.

There is nothing higher than Goodness. We can't imagine anything more beautiful than Goodness. When people see Perfect Goodness, they call it God. When they see Goodness in a person, they worship him as God.

We see Jesus as a sinless man; in him, Perfect Goodness is clearly shown, not in a complicated or mysterious way, but through his words and actions. Because of his sinlessness, he is accepted as a role model and teacher for all.

There have been few great Teachers throughout history. Hundreds of years may pass without the appearance of such a person. But when a True Teacher does appear, we recognize them by the way they live. Their actions are different from others, and their teachings come from their own life, not from any book or person. The Teacher lives first and then teaches others how to live. The proof of their teaching is found in their own life. Out of millions of preachers, only one is truly accepted by humanity as a Teacher, and that one is the person who truly lives. The others are just talkers and explainers, and they quickly fade away from human memory.

Jesus, as a Teacher, lived the perfect life of Divine Love, even under the hardest circumstances. He lived a life of Goodwill, which is different from the self-centered life that most people choose. There was no selfishness in him; all his thoughts, words, and actions came from the spirit of Love. He gave himself so completely to this spirit of Love that he became one with it, so much that he literally became Love in human form. He achieved complete victory over his own desires by obeying the Divine Law of Love within himself, and through this obedience, he became divine. His entire teaching is that anyone who practices the same obedience can also experience this divine Life and become consciously divine.

The never-ending kindness, compassion, forgiveness, love, and patience of Jesus are the subjects of countless hymns and millions of heartfelt prayers. This is because these qualities are recognized by everyone as being truly divine. Making these qualities the main goal of your life is what Religion is all about. On the other hand, denying these qualities and continuing to live in their opposites—pride, judgment, harshness, hate, and anger—is what irreligion is.

Deep down, people everywhere know that Goodness is divine, even if they argue against it. Jesus is worshipped as God, not because he claimed it or because of any miracles in his life, but because he never strayed from Perfect Goodness and Faultless Love. "God is Love," and Love is God. People know no other God except Love shown in the human heart and life through pure thoughts, kind words, and compassionate actions. And we can only know this God to the extent that we have experienced Love within ourselves by overcoming our selfishness. The God that people argue about in theology, whose existence or non-existence is debated, is a God of theories and speculation. The person who, by overcoming their own selfishness, has found the Supreme Love within themselves, knows what Love is beyond any argument, and this Love can only be lived. Such a person lives it, leaving empty arguments to those who refuse to rise higher.

After fully living the Divine Life through obedience, Jesus gave the world simple spiritual rules that, if followed, could help all people become sons of God and live the Perfect Life. These rules are so straightforward and clear that they can't be misunderstood. They are so plain that even a young child can understand them. All these rules focus on how we behave, and they can only be applied by each individual in their own life. Living by these rules in our daily actions is the whole duty of life and helps each person realize their divine nature and oneness with God, the Supreme Good. However, this is where the difficulty comes in. While millions of people worship

Jesus as God in a miraculous or mystical way, very few actually believe in his teachings or try to follow them in their own lives. The rules themselves are not hard to understand or follow; the problem is that many people simply don't believe it is possible to live by them, so they never try. Others believe it is possible but are not willing to make the personal sacrifices that these rules require. But without honestly trying to live by the teachings of Jesus, there can be no true life. Simply calling Jesus "Lord" does not make someone his disciple. True discipleship means weaving his words into the fabric of your life and practicing his divine teachings of self-perfection.

Let it be clear from the beginning that I have nothing to do with the many creeds that have been built around the Hebrew Scriptures. My focus is entirely on the life and teachings of Jesus and the deep truths of the human heart that his teachings aim to reach. I care about Goodness, not about speculation; about Love, not about theological debates; about self-perfection, not fleeting opinions.

Jesus was an extremely good man; this is something everyone knows, and knowing this is all we need. He left us teachings that, if followed, will lead anyone directly to the Supreme Goodness. Knowing this is both joyful and inspiring.

A good person is the best of humanity, and to grow purer, nobler, and more God-like every day by overcoming selfish desires is to constantly draw closer to the Divine Heart. "If anyone wants to be my disciple, they must deny themselves daily," is a statement that no one can misunderstand, even if they choose to ignore it. Nowhere in the universe is there anything that can replace Goodness, and until someone possesses it, they have nothing of real value. The only way to achieve Goodness is to give up everything that stands in its way. Every selfish desire must be removed, every impure thought must be let go of, and every attachment to opinion must be sacrificed. Doing this is what it means to follow Christ. Above all beliefs and opinions is a loving and self-sacrificing heart. The life of Jesus demonstrates this truth, and all of his teachings are designed to help us reach this holy and supreme goal.

To live in love always and toward everyone is to live the true life, to have Life itself. Jesus lived this way, and anyone can live this way if they humbly and faithfully follow his teachings. As long as people refuse to do this and hold onto their desires, passions, and opinions, they cannot truly be his disciples; they are only disciples of themselves. "Truly, I say to you: anyone who continues to sin is a servant of sin," is one of Jesus's most powerful statements. People should stop deceiving themselves into thinking they can hold onto their bad tempers, lusts, harsh words, judgments, personal hatreds, petty arguments, and favorite opinions, and still have Christ. Anything that divides people or separates them from Goodness is not from Christ, because Christ is Love.

To keep sinning is to be a doer of sin, a follower of self, not a doer of righteousness or a follower of Christ. Sin and Christ cannot exist together, and anyone who accepts the Christ-life of pure Goodness will stop sinning. Following Christ means giving up everything in our mind and behavior that goes against the spirit of Love. This, as we will see, requires complete self-surrender and a refusal to hold onto any thought that isn't pure, compassionate, and gentle. The Christ-spirit of Love ends all sin, as well as all division and conflict. If I argue about whether Jesus is divine or not, and my opinion creates division, I have already lost the spirit of Christ, which is Love. When Christ becomes a topic of argument, Christ is lost.

It is just as selfish and sinful to hold onto an opinion as it is to hold onto an impure desire. Knowing this, the good person gives themselves completely to the spirit of Love, living in Love toward everyone, arguing with no one, condemning no one, hating no one, but loving all. They see past others' opinions, beliefs, and sins and look into their struggling, suffering hearts. "Whoever loves their life will lose it." Eternal Life belongs to the person who is willing to give up their small, selfish, sinful self because only by doing this can they enter the large, beautiful, free, and joyful life of Love. This is the Path of Life, for the narrow Gate is the Gate of Goodness, and the narrow Way is the Way of self-sacrifice. The Gate is so narrow that no sin can pass through, and the Way is so narrow that anyone walking it can bring no selfish thoughts along as companions.

Chapter 2
The Law and the Prophets

Do to others whatever you would like them to
do to you; this is the essence of the Law and
he Prophets.—Jesus

If you want to enter into life, keep the
Commandments.—Jesus

The commandments and teachings of Jesus were given
for people to follow. This is such a simple and obvious
truth that it shouldn't even need to be stated. Yet, after
nearly 1,900 years of his teachings being in the world,
it's clear that it still needs to be said, as many people
believe that following these teachings is not only
impractical but completely impossible for humans to do.
This belief, rooted in ignorance, is the first
misconception that keeps people from understanding
spiritual truths. It's impossible for anyone to truly grasp
spiritual things until they get rid of this false belief.

The words of Jesus come from a deep
understanding of divine Law, and everything he said is
in perfect harmony with eternal Truth. People realize

this as they bring the spiritual life contained in his words into their own lives—that is, as they begin living by his teachings.

Let's take a look at these teachings and explore how to put them into practice, and what they mean. Most of them are found in the Sermon on the Mount, and all of them focus on personal behavior. This leaves us with only two options: either to live by them or to ignore them.

I don't need to go through each teaching one by one since my readers already have the Bible, and each teaching is based on the same divine principle. To understand the spirit of one is to understand the spirit of them all. In fact, all of Jesus' teachings, and the entire purpose of life in both human and divine relationships, are summed up in these 17 words: "Do to others what you would want them to do to you." It's only necessary to look at the other teachings to help explain how to live by this one because, in understanding this one rule, you understand the entire scope of spiritual life and knowledge. "This is the Law and the Prophets."

This teaching is incredibly simple, which is why people have had such a hard time understanding and applying it. But living by this teaching leaves no room for selfishness, and following it completely means reaching Christ-like perfection in character. However, before anyone can practice it, they must first understand it, and even this first step requires a level of self-surrender that few are willing to make. No one can learn anything unless they approach it with the attitude of a learner. Before anyone can learn anything from the divine spirit within, they must come to Christ with an open heart, free from their desires, opinions, and even their most cherished beliefs, like a little child who knows nothing, blind and seeking knowledge. Without this humble attitude, it's impossible to achieve divine life and knowledge. But the person who takes this attitude will quickly begin to experience the highest spiritual revelations, and living by this teaching will soon become natural and easy.

Once someone humbles themselves, the first questions they ask are: "How am I treating others?" "What am I doing for others?" "How do I think about others?" "Are my thoughts and actions toward others motivated by unselfish love, as I would want theirs to be toward me? Or are they driven by personal dislike, petty revenge, or narrow-minded bigotry and judgment?" As a person asks themselves these soul-searching questions, applying all their thoughts and actions to the spirit of Jesus' primary teaching, their understanding will be enlightened. They will clearly see where they've gone wrong and what they need to do to change their heart and behavior. Such a person has become a disciple of Christ, sitting at his feet and ready to follow his commands, no matter the personal cost.

Spending just one hour each day meditating on this teaching, combined with a sincere desire to understand it and a determination to live by it, would quickly lift someone out of their sinful nature into the clear light and freedom of divine Truth. This would force them to transform their entire life and change how they relate to others. Before acting, a person should ask themselves, "Would I want someone else to do this to me?" By doing so, they'll soon find their way out of spiritual darkness and begin living for others instead of for themselves. Their thoughts and behavior will align with the Principle of divine Love, instead of following their selfish desires. No matter how others treat them, they'll start treating everyone with calm, quiet, forgiving love. If others attack their beliefs, their religion, or their way of life, they won't retaliate. They'll stop attacking others because they'll realize their highest duty is to follow their divine Master's teachings. Living by those teachings will require them to not only change their thoughts and actions but also every aspect of their life, down to what they eat, drink, and wear.

As they progress in this new way of life, the teachings of Jesus will shine with new light and energy. They will feel that every teaching is meant for them and that they must live by them, no longer accusing others for not doing the same. When they read the words "Do not judge," they will know they must stop judging others harshly and unkindly. They'll learn to think kindly of everyone, treating those who are unkind to them just as kindly as those who treat them well. Even if others judge or condemn them, they won't do the same in return. They'll set aside personal feelings and deal with everyone with fairness, wisdom, and love. By following this simple teaching, "Do not judge," a person will rise above selfishness and personal biases, developing deep spiritual strength. This new way of life will naturally lead to following the teaching, "Do not resist evil," because if a person stops judging others as evil, they'll stop resisting them as evil.

In recent years, a lot has been said about not resisting evil, but to understand the spiritual meaning of this, or any teaching, a person must go beyond intellectual arguments and actually practice it. They can only understand it by doing it. By practicing this teaching, a person will destroy the habit of seeing evil in the world, and they'll begin to see the good and the truth instead. They'll realize that evil is not worth resisting and that living a life of goodness is far more important.

When a person is focused on resisting evil, they aren't actually practicing goodness. In fact, they're caught up in the same passions and prejudices they condemn in others. As a result, they find themselves being resisted by others in the same way. If someone fights against another person, a group, a law, a religion, or a government, believing it to be evil, they'll soon find themselves being fought against as evil. If a person wants to stop being persecuted or condemned, they should stop persecuting and condemning others. They should turn away from everything they've been resisting as evil and start looking for the good. By removing passion, resentment, and revenge from their heart, they'll quickly realize that the evil they've been fighting against doesn't truly exist. It was just an exaggerated reflection of the passion and foolishness within themselves. This teaching is so profound that practicing it will take a person far along the path of spiritual understanding. When they've purified themselves enough to see good in everyone and everything, they'll be ready to live by an even higher teaching, "Love your enemies."

Many people stumble over this teaching, and the reason why is clear. It's natural that people who see fighting, revenge, and hatred toward their enemies as signs of strength would view this teaching as not only impractical but foolish. From their perspective, they're right. If we see humans as merely animals, separated from the Divine, then the aggressive, destructive qualities that are considered noble in animals would also be considered noble in humans.

To people living according to their animal instincts, meekness, forgiveness, and selfless love seem like weakness, cowardice, and foolishness. However, if we recognize that humans possess divine qualities, such as love, purity, compassion, reason, and wisdom— qualities that lift them above animals—then the teaching to "Love your enemies" not only seems possible but represents the true, rightful state of humanity. To someone who says, "This teaching is impossible," I would say, "You're right, it's impossible for you. But it's only your lack of belief in the power of Goodness, and your belief in the strength of animal instincts, that makes it seem that way. Change your mindset, and what seemed impossible will become possible."

No one can live by this teaching without being willing to give up their animal nature. Anyone who wants to find Christ, the pure spirit of Truth, must stop clouding their spiritual vision by indulging their emotions and passions. The source of all hatred within themselves must be eliminated. Hatred is still hatred, even if we call it dislike. Personal dislikes, no matter how natural they seem to the animal man, have no place in the divine life. And as long as someone's mind is filled with malice, dislike, animosity, revenge, or the arrogance of thinking "I'm right, and you're wrong," they cannot understand spiritual truths.

Keeping the commandment, "Love your enemies," requires removing all hatred and arrogance from the heart. As this happens, the Principle of Divine Love, which is unchanging toward everyone—whether they're just or unjust, sinful or saintly—replaces the volatile, personal loves that are linked to their opposites of intense hatred. It's impossible to love one's enemies while living in the animal personality because that personality is rooted in both blind love and hatred. It's only by abandoning the personal, selfish mindset that the impersonal, divine Love—which doesn't change based on how others treat us—can take over. When that happens, the disciple realizes that their true nature is divine.

The Love that enables a person to be kind to their enemies, and to treat others the way they want to be treated, regardless of how others behave, isn't a fleeting emotion or preference. It's a state of divine understanding reached through practice. As this understanding deepens, the eternal principles of Divine Law, which the Prophets spoke of, are fully understood.

Anyone who follows the teachings of Jesus will conquer themselves and become spiritually enlightened. Those who do not follow them will remain trapped in the darkness of their lower nature, unable to understand spiritual truths or the Divine Law. This is also the ultimate test of discipleship, for it was Jesus Christ himself who said, "Whoever does not love me does not keep my teachings," and "Whoever has my commandments and keeps them is the one who loves me."

Chapter 3
The Yoke and the Burden

Take my teachings upon you and learn from
Me, because I am gentle and humble in heart;
and you will find peace for your soul. For my
teachings are simple, and my guidance is light.
—Jesus

So be perfect, just as your Father in Heaven is
perfect. —Jesus

Humanity is naturally divine. Every teaching of Jesus is
based on this truth. If people weren't divine, his
teachings would have no meaning because there would
be nothing within them (no divine spirit) that could
respond to his message. The fact that humans are
capable of loving their enemies and returning good for
evil proves their inner, divine nature. If sin were man's
natural state, then staying in it would be right, and there
wouldn't be any reason to encourage people to live
virtuously, because they wouldn't be able to act against
their original nature. Every time people encourage
others to act with virtue, kindness, purity, and
unselfishness, they unknowingly affirm humanity's

divine nature, showing that humans are above sin and have the power to overcome it.

However, humanity has lived in sin for so long that people now see themselves as naturally sinful and cut off from the Divine Source, which they believe is outside of them. As a result, they've lost the awareness and understanding of their own divinity, of their true unity with God, the Spirit of Good. Right now, humanity is like the Prodigal Son, wandering in the distant land of sin and trying to survive on the empty desires and false beliefs of the world. Every divine command is a call for people to return to their Father's House, to their Original Innocence, and to regain their awareness of their oneness with the Divine.

The entire teaching of Jesus is a call for people to live as he did, to follow his example. By doing so, he acknowledges and affirms humanity's inherent equality with himself. When he says, "I and my Father are One," he speaks not just for himself but for all people. The difference between the life of Jesus and the lives of others is not something imposed on them, nor is it an essential difference; it is self-imposed and comes from individual choices. Jesus fully recognized his oneness with the Father (the Divine Source) and lived consciously in that unity. Other people, generally speaking, not only don't recognize their oneness with the Divine, but they don't believe in it. Because of their lack of belief, they cannot rise to the dignity and majesty of the Divine Life. As long as someone sees themselves as a creature of sin, believing they are naturally degraded, they will remain that way, enslaved by sin. But when they realize they are originally divine, that they never were and never can be separated from the Divine except by their own ignorance and choices, they will rise above sin and begin to express the Divine Life.

Man is fundamentally a spiritual being and, as such, is made of the same substance as the Eternal Spirit, the Unchanging Reality, which people call God. Goodness, not sin, is man's true state; perfection, not imperfection, is his inheritance. A person can enter into this realization right now if they accept the condition, which is the denial or letting go of self. This means letting go of selfish desires, pride, egotism, and self-interest—all the things St. Paul called the "natural man."

In the Sermon on the Mount, Jesus explains the way of living and thinking by which the divine life can be experienced. After laying out the entire duty of humans as spiritual beings, as children of God, he encourages people to live according to their divine nature by saying, "Be perfect, just as your Father in Heaven is perfect." When Jesus calls people to perfection, he isn't asking for the impossible. He's simply urging them to live their true life of divine perfection and to give up their false life of self-interest and sin.

The "yoke" that Jesus asks people to take on is the yoke of obedience—obedience to the divine nature that is within everyone, instead of following lower desires and impulses. The "burden" is the burden of living a sinless life. This yoke is "easy" because it brings no suffering, and this burden is "light" because it's free from sorrow, anxiety, and fear. It's the life of self-interest that's difficult and burdensome, while the weight of sin, even in its mildest forms, is heavy and tiring. Anyone can see this truth by looking around at the world and then looking within their own soul.

Jesus saw the divine in everyone, even those considered "evil," and he continually emphasized this truth. The idea that humans are naturally degraded, as lost creatures unable to rise to the heights of Goodness and Righteousness, is nowhere to be found in the words or teachings of Jesus. Instead, his entire message affirms humanity's inherent Goodness and their unlimited ability to practice it. When he says, "Don't condemn, and you won't be condemned; forgive, and you'll be forgiven; give, and it will be given to you," he's telling us that if we let go of resentment and treat others with kindness, forgiveness, and gentle consideration, we'll discover that people are so naturally good that they'll return kindness in abundance. If someone wants to see how good people really are, they should stop focusing on the "evil" in others and start practicing the good within themselves.

Jesus also spoke about the "righteous," those who "hunger and thirst for righteousness," the "meek," the "merciful," the "pure in heart," and the "peacemakers," and said that all such people are blessed. He points out that even those who see themselves as sinful still know how to give good gifts to their children, and that even publicans and sinners return love for love. His message about the innocence of little children seems to have been largely overlooked by those who claim to follow him. In all his interactions with and references to those who had fallen, Jesus looked past the surface appearance of sin, which others see as the real person and often exaggerate, and instead saw the divine beauty and goodness hidden beneath the layers of sin.

He described sinners as "captives" and "blind," saying his mission was to free them and restore their sight. This clearly shows that sin is not a natural part of man, and that sinlessness is his true state. Jesus even said that people would do greater works than he did.

Nowhere in all of history or spiritual writings is there such a powerful testimony to the nobility, purity, and Goodness of the human heart as in the words and deeds of Jesus. In his divine Goodness, he understood the human heart and knew that it was good.

People have within them the divine power to rise to the highest spiritual achievements. They can shake off sin, shame, and sorrow and do the will of the Father, the Supreme Good. They can conquer all the darkness within and stand radiant and free. They can overcome the world and reach the highest levels of Truth. But they can only do this through obedience. They must choose meekness and humility. They must let go of strife in exchange for peace, passion for purity, hatred for love, and self-interest for self-sacrifice. They must overcome evil with good, for this is the holy Way of Truth. This is the safe and enduring salvation. This is the yoke and burden of Christ.

Chapter 4
The Word and the Doer

Whoever hears my words and follows them is
like a wise man who built his house on solid
rock. When the rain came, and the floods rose,
and the winds blew and struck the house, it did
not fall because it was built on a strong
foundation.—Jesus

If you continue to follow my teachings, you are
truly my disciples, and you will know the
Truth, and the Truth will set you free.—Jesus

The message of Jesus is about living and doing. If it
wasn't, it wouldn't express eternal truth. His way of life
is about pure behavior, and the way to enter it is
through giving up selfishness. It tells people to stop
sinning, and in return, it offers joy, happiness, and
perfect peace.

One thing all great teachers, who are worshipped as
saviors, have in common is that they reveal and speak
to the simple truths of the soul and life. This quality
stands out the most in Jesus' teachings. He didn't create

any theories, push any beliefs, or claim any special opinions. He didn't come up with any complicated philosophy. He simply told the truth.

People are often caught up in their pleasures, theories, religions, and philosophies, so they can't understand the simple truths of life. The real job of a true teacher is to help people return to the simple and beautiful truths of their own souls. The false teacher, who cannot see the basic truths of duty and behavior, but doesn't see himself and others clearly, will tell people that the truth can only be found in accepting his personal beliefs, warning them against other ideas. But the true teacher, who knows the human heart and sees life as it is, doesn't do this. Especially Jesus, who, when asked about the Way of Life, always told people to go and do certain things. He never referred them to his personal opinions, theories, or clever philosophies, nor those of other people. He always pointed them towards duty and pure living and behavior. The only thing he warned people against were their own sins. And this is all that's necessary. A person either gives up sin or holds on to it; if they give it up, they do everything they need to and understand the Law of Life; if they hold on to it, they do nothing and stay ignorant, blind, and without understanding.

Truth is in behavior, not in any system of ideas. To live purely and blamelessly is far better than any set of ideas. Let a person study every religion, and in the end, they will find that one selfless thought or one pure action is better than them all. Truth has nothing to do with religious arguments, but it shines brightly in an unselfish action. This is beautifully shown in the parables of Jesus and in many events of his life, especially in the story in Luke, chapter 10, where a lawyer asks, "Teacher, what must I do to have eternal life?" Jesus' answer was to ask him to repeat the greatest commandment, and after he did, Jesus said, "Do this, and you will live." The lawyer, wanting to pull Jesus into an argument, asked, "And who is my neighbor?"

This leads to the famous story of the Good Samaritan, where Jesus uses simple words and images to clearly show that religious acts are worthless unless they're done with kindness, and that a so-called worldly person who does unselfish deeds has already found eternal life, while the religious person who refuses to be kind and unselfish is far from life. To fully understand this parable, you need to know that priests and Levites were considered highly favored by God, while Samaritans were seen as completely outside the possibility of being saved.

Jesus didn't believe in any religion except behavior; and truly, there is no other. Pure goodness is true religion, and without it, there is no religion. There are many beliefs, and there's a lot of arguing about them, but a person is only truly religious when they rise above these things and reach the place in their heart where all hateful differences are burned away by pure compassion and love. Jesus lived in this divine place, and he calls others to join him there to find rest and peace.

That Jesus was humble, loving, compassionate, and pure is wonderful, but it's not enough. Reader, you must also be humble, loving, compassionate, and pure. That Jesus gave up his own will to follow God's will is inspiring, but it's not enough. You must also give up your will to follow the greater good. The grace, beauty, and goodness in Jesus are worthless to you, cannot be understood by you, unless they are also in you. They will never be in you unless you practice them, because without action, goodness doesn't exist for you. Worshiping Jesus for his divine qualities is a great step toward truth, but practicing those qualities is truth itself. Anyone who truly admires the perfection of another will not be satisfied with their own imperfections but will shape their soul to become like the one they admire. None of us can find enough joy, peace, or happiness in the goodness of another, not even the goodness of God. It's only when we act with goodness, when we put in constant effort to make goodness a part of our being, that we can experience its joy and peace. So, if you admire Jesus for his divine qualities, practice those qualities yourself, and you too will become divine.

The teachings of Jesus bring people back to the simple truth that righteousness, or right actions, is entirely based on individual behavior. It's not some mystical thing separate from a person's thoughts and actions. Each person must be righteous for themselves; each must act on the word of truth. It's a person's own actions that bring peace and happiness, not the actions of another.

Millions of people worship Jesus and call him Lord, but Jesus doesn't leave any confusion about who his true disciples are or who has entered into life. His words are as clear as they can be: "Not everyone who says to me, Lord, Lord, will enter the kingdom of heaven, but only those who do the will of my Father in heaven." And again, "Why do you call me Lord, Lord, and not do what I say?" The true followers are those who live their lives according to the divine instructions.

The doer of the word proves its truth in their own mind and life. In this way, they know the Eternal Rock as a solid reality inside themselves, and they build on it the Temple of Righteousness, which no grief, temptation, or sin can destroy or weaken. It's only those who forgive who experience the joy of forgiveness. It's only those who practice love, mercy, and righteousness who receive the full blessings of these qualities in their hearts. Only those who live in peace with everyone can know the limitless peace. This is why the doer of the word is a true disciple, and by living according to the word, becoming one with it in heart and mind, they know the truth that sets the soul free from the chains of sin.

Chapter 5
The Vine and the Branches

I am the Vine, and you are the branches.
Whoever stays connected to Me, and I to them,
will produce much fruit. Without Me, you can't
do anything.—Jesus

Come to Me, all of you who are tired and
carrying heavy burdens, and I will give you
rest.—Jesus

Christ is the Spirit of Love, which is the constant and real presence in every person. Though its perfect home is the human body, and it can only truly show itself through the human personality, it is universal, eternal, and not tied to any one person. It is both the source of life and life itself.

In this Spirit of Love, all Knowledge, Intelligence, and Wisdom exist. Until a person recognizes it as the most important truth within them, they do not fully understand Christ. This beautiful understanding is the peak of personal growth and the ultimate purpose of life. Achieving this is complete salvation—freedom from all mistakes, ignorance, and sin.

This principle is within everyone, but not everyone shows it. The reason people don't recognize or show it is that they hold onto personal desires that block its power and presence. Every personal desire is temporary and will pass away, and holding onto them is holding onto illusions, shadows, and death. In the material world, you can't see an object until you remove the obstacles in front of it. In the spiritual world, you can't understand a lasting Principle until you let go of all temporary things. Before someone can know Love as the lasting reality within them, they must completely give up all human tendencies that block its perfect expression. By doing this, they become one with Love—become Love itself—and realize that they have always been divine and one with God.

Jesus, by completely overcoming his personal self, realized and showed his unity with the Supreme Spirit. By giving his whole life to impersonal Love, he became a true embodiment of Christ. That's why he is rightly called the Christ.

When Jesus said, "Without Me you can do nothing," he wasn't talking about his physical body but the Universal Spirit of Love that his actions perfectly showed. This statement is simply true because any action done for personal reasons is empty and meaningless. A person stays caught in darkness and fear of death as long as they live for their own selfish pleasures. The animal part of a person can never understand the divine; only the divine can connect with the divine. The spirit of hate in a person can never understand the Spirit of Love; only Love can understand Love and join with it. Humans are divine, made from Love itself, and they can realize this if they let go of the selfish, personal desires they've been following and turn to the impersonal Realities of the Christ Spirit, which are Purity, Humility, Compassion, Wisdom, and Love.

Every command from Jesus requires the complete sacrifice of some selfish, personal desire before it can be followed. A person cannot know the Real while clinging to the unreal, and they cannot do the work of Truth while holding onto falsehood. As long as someone holds onto lust, hate, pride, vanity, greed, or selfishness, they can do nothing, for the works of these sinful desires are false and temporary.

Only when a person turns to the Spirit of Love within and becomes patient, kind, pure, merciful, and forgiving can they do the works of Righteousness and bear the fruits of Life. The vine is not complete without its branches, and it isn't truly whole until those branches bear fruit. Love is not complete until it is lived by people, understood by them, and shown through their actions.

A person can only connect themselves to the Vine of Love by giving up all conflict, hate, judgment, impurity, pride, and selfishness and by thinking only loving thoughts and doing loving actions. By doing this, they awaken the divine nature within that they have been denying and rejecting.

Every time a person gives in to anger, impatience, greed, pride, vanity, or any form of selfishness, they deny Christ and shut themselves off from Love. This is the only way Christ is denied—not by refusing to accept a certain belief. Christ is only known to the person who, through constant effort, transforms themselves from a sinful being into a pure one. By making a strong moral effort, they let go of the temporary self, which is the source of all suffering, sorrow, and restlessness, and become reasonable, kind, peaceful, loving, and pure.

A person's only escape from sin is sinless Love. By turning to this Love, living in it, letting go of everything else as temporary, false, and worthless, and practicing love towards all people in thought, mind, and action, with no harmful or impure thoughts, they discover the eternal Principles of their being. They fully realize their unity with eternal Life and experience never-ending peace.

Chapter 6
Salvation This Day

Salvation has come to this house today.
Jesus to Zacchaeus

The Kingdom of God is within you.
Jesus

I have tried to show in the previous sections that the teachings of Jesus are entirely based on perfect behavior and can be summed up in one word: Goodness. Jesus showed this Goodness in his life, and his teachings are powerful because they are rooted in his actions and behavior. His command to "Follow me" is meant to be taken literally and practically, not as a copy of the specific details of his life, but by rising (as he did) to the heights of Goodness, Compassion, and Love through conquering the self. The beauty of his teachings is contained in his principles, and the greatness of his life is found in them. Whoever follows these principles in their life will perfect their behavior by purifying the inner thoughts and actions, becoming a spiritual and sinless being who fulfills the purpose of life. This is also where complete salvation is found, meaning freedom from sin.

Jesus only used the word "salvation" twice, and only one of those times (when speaking to Zacchaeus) has real meaning for us. In that one short statement, we fully understand its meaning because it directly relates to the changed behavior of Zacchaeus. Before meeting Jesus, Zacchaeus had been harsh, greedy, and selfish. Even though he hadn't met the new Teacher in person yet, he had heard the message that a person can and should repent, stop selfish and sinful behavior, and live a life of goodness and kindness. Zacchaeus had done this, and having experienced its happiness, he joyfully welcomed Jesus into his home. He told him how he had stopped doing wrong and started doing right, how he had traded evil for good, selfishness for kindness. Jesus didn't ask Zacchaeus about his "religious beliefs," didn't ask him to change his opinions, and didn't demand that he believe anything about Jesus being the Messiah or the Son of God. Zacchaeus had changed his behavior. He had completely shifted his attitude toward others, exchanging greed for generosity, dishonesty for honesty, selfishness for unselfishness, evil for good—and this was enough, as Jesus said in the words, "This day salvation has come to this house."

The only salvation Jesus taught is salvation from sin and its effects, here and now. A person must give up their old selfishness and old way of living in any and every form. Only by doing this and turning to a new life of kindness, purity, humility, and unselfish love can someone be said to be saved from sin. Then they are truly saved, because once they stop practicing sin, it no longer troubles them. This is also where Heaven is found, not as an imagined place after death, but as a real, constant Heaven in the heart. It's a Heaven where all selfish desires and painful emotions are gone, where Love rules, and where Peace is always present.

The message of Jesus is truly good news because it reveals to people their divine potential. It tells those who are suffering from sin, "Take up your bed and walk." It shows that a person doesn't have to remain trapped in darkness, ignorance, and sin if they believe in Goodness and strive to overcome until they have made that Goodness a reality in their life. By believing and overcoming, a person not only has the perfect rule of Jesus' teachings to guide them, but they also have the inner guide, the Spirit of Truth within their own heart, "The Light that shines in every person coming into the world," which, as they follow it, will show them the divine origin of those teachings.

Whoever humbly passes through the Gate of Good, resolving to give up everything in their nature that is not pure, true, or loving, and vowing to stop every violation of the Divine principles, will be rewarded. To that person, who is faithful, humble, and true, the amazing

Vision of the Perfect One will be revealed. As they purify their heart and perfect their behavior according to this vision, they will rise above the weaknesses of their lower nature, cleanse every stain from their soul, and realize the perfect goodness of the eternal Christ.

Thank you for Reading

You've Just Read a Piece of the Greatest Library Ever Rebuilt

Thank you for reading.

This book is one of thousands we're restoring, reimagining, and translating as part of the **Modern Library of Alexandria** — a global movement to preserve and share humanity's most important ideas.

What was once lost to fire and time is now rising again — not just as memory, but as living, breathing knowledge, freely accessible to all.

What You Can Do Next:

- **Keep Reading.**

  Discover more legendary works — in beautiful print, audiobook, or digital form — at LibraryofAlexandria.com.

- **Build Your Own Library.**

  Every title is available as a paperback, hardcover, or collectible boxset — at true printing cost. Craft a personal library worthy of display.

- **Spread the Light.**

  Share this book. Tell others about the movement. Help us translate every timeless work into every language, so no reader is ever left behind.

By finishing this book, you've already taken part in something extraordinary.

Join us at LibraryofAlexandria.com

Together, we're rebuilding the greatest library the world has ever known.

With appreciation,
The Modern Library of Alexandria Team

Visit:

www.libraryofalexandria.com

Or scan the code below: